# ECOGRAPHICS

# CLIMATE CHANGE

Izzi Howell

W

Franklin Watts

First published in paperback in Great Britain in 2019 by The Watts Publishing Group

Produced for Franklin Watts by
White-Thomson Publishing Ltd
www.wtpub.co.uk
01273 479982

Editor: Izzi Howell
Designer: Clare Nicholas
Cover designer: Steve Mead

Getty: helt2 6, Per-Anders Pettersson 15b, FRISO GENTSCH/AF 17, sal73it 19b, Robert_Ford 21t, Photographer, Videographer, Writer 25l, Lemanieh 25r, Karl Spencer 26t; National Snow and Ice Data Center: Nick Cobbing/Greenpeace 13t; Shutterstock: Designua 9, FloridaStock 11t, Sk Hasan Ali 11b, Red monkey 12, gary yim 13b, Earl D. Walker 15t, Artisticco 18, Amanda Nicholls 19t, Tomacco 20, hikrcn 21b, testing 23, ProStockStudio 24, GraphicsRF 26, AMFPhotography 26b.

All design elements from Shutterstock.

ISBN 978 1 4451 6572 1

Printed in Dubai

Franklin Watts
An imprint of
Hachette Children's Group
Part of The Watts Publishing Group
Carmelite House
50 Victoria Embankment
London EC4Y 0DZ

An Hachette UK Company
www.hachette.co.uk
www.franklinwatts.co.uk

# Contents

# What is climate change?

Temperature changes are normal on Earth. Throughout our planet's 4.5 billion year history, there have been periods of cooler and warmer temperatures, which have happened naturally. However, the Earth is now warmer than at any point over the last 650,000 years. Most scientists agree that this climate change is not natural and is caused by human activity.

## Causes

methane gas released by livestock (page 14)

some fertilisers (page 8)

burning fossil fuels (page 6)

deforestation (page 14)

burning biomass (wood, plants)

**97%** of climate scientists agree that the current changes in climate are due to human activity.

By 2050, **200 million** people may have had to leave their homes because of climate change.

## Threats

Climate change is a huge threat to life on Earth. Its effect on the natural environment could result in the destruction of many habitats and the extinction of some plants and animals. It is also affecting the places where humans live and our food supply.

desertification (page 20)

rising temperatures (page 9)

wildfires

melting polar ice (page 10)

flooding (page 11)

extreme weather (page 24)

habitat loss

animal extinction

## Stopping climate change

As humans are the cause of climate change, it is also our responsibility to stop it from happening. Most of the activity that causes climate change comes from industry. However, we can all make changes to help slow down or stop climate change, from planting trees to using renewable electricity sources.

# Fossil fuels

Oil, natural gas and coal are all examples of fossil fuels. They are burned to power factories and vehicles, and to create electricity. The use of fossil fuels is a major cause of climate change.

## Sources

Fossil fuels come from under the ground. They formed over millions of years from the remains of dead plants and animals. Oil and natural gas are pumped out of the ground through deep narrow holes. Coal is mined below ground and at the Earth's surface.

oil pump

oil

coal

## Burning fossil fuels

When fossil fuels are burned, they give off heat energy. This heat energy is used to create power. However, burning fossil fuels also gives off carbon dioxide ($CO_2$). Carbon dioxide is a greenhouse gas (see page 8), which contributes to climate change.

**Burning coal is the single largest cause of climate change.**

*A coal-powered power plant in the USA releases carbon dioxide and pollution into the air.*

## Going, going, gone

Since the beginning of the Industrial Revolution in the eighteenth century, we have used huge amounts of fossil fuels. The amount of oil, natural gas and coal left on Earth is running low. Population increase means that we are using more fossil fuels than ever before. If we continue to use fossil fuels at the same rate or faster, we may run out in the next hundred years.

## Making a change

Many people are starting to choose alternative energy sources now (see panel below), before fossil fuels run out forever. Leaving fossil fuels in the ground and changing over to different energy sources will help to slow down the rate of climate change.

## Fossil fuel dependent

Some less economically developed countries depend on fossil fuels for their economy. They can't afford to switch to alternative energy sources. Without fossil fuels, they couldn't produce enough income to support their citizens and develop their country further. However, these less economically developed countries also tend to be near the equator, and are some of the most affected by climate change.

## One small step

See if your school can install a solar panel. You might have to raise the money to buy and fit the panel, but after it's in place, your school will save money on bills within a few years and use fewer fossil fuels.

## Alternative energy

We can use power from the Sun, the wind and moving water to create electricity. As these natural power sources will never run out, we don't need to worry about our supply ending, as we do with fossil fuels. They also don't create any greenhouse gases, so they have no negative impact on climate change.

# Global warming

Global warming is a part of climate change. The average temperature on Earth is increasing because of the greenhouse effect. This is a natural process that traps heat from the Sun close to the Earth.

## Greenhouse gases

The greenhouse effect is caused by certain gases, which are known as greenhouse gases. Greenhouse gases are produced both naturally and by human activity.

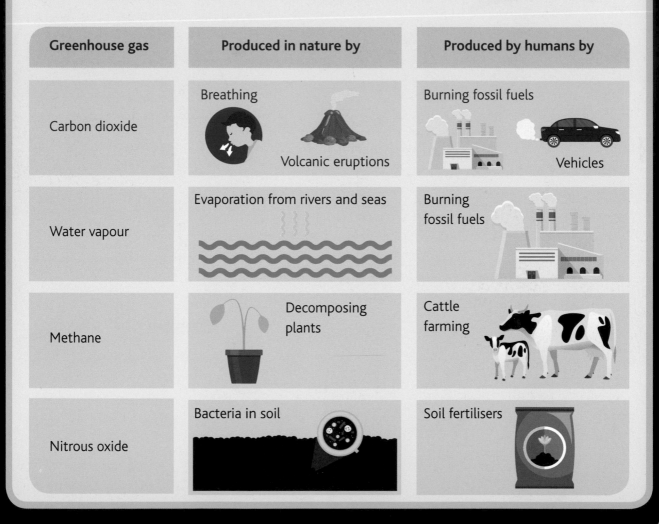

| Greenhouse gas | Produced in nature by | Produced by humans by |
| --- | --- | --- |
| Carbon dioxide | Breathing<br>Volcanic eruptions | Burning fossil fuels<br>Vehicles |
| Water vapour | Evaporation from rivers and seas | Burning fossil fuels |
| Methane | Decomposing plants | Cattle farming |
| Nitrous oxide | Bacteria in soil | Soil fertilisers |

## The atmosphere

The Earth is surrounded by an atmosphere – a layer of gases that stretches from directly above the ground to 10,000 km into space. The Earth's atmosphere blocks harmful radiation from the Sun, but lets through light and heat. After greenhouse gases are produced, they collect in the atmosphere above the Earth's surface.

## Trapped heat

During the day, light and heat from the Sun pass through the atmosphere and warm the Earth's surface. At night, heat from the surface should travel back out into the air as the Earth cools down. However, some of the heat is trapped close to the Earth by greenhouse gases in the atmosphere. This makes the temperature on the surface increase.

Global warming doesn't just result in hotter weather. It can also cause more rain and snow in some areas (see pages 24–25).

## Warm but not too hot

**-18°C**

The greenhouse effect is necessary for life on Earth. Without it, the average temperature on Earth would be around -18°C – far too cold for most plants and animals to survive. However, the large amounts of greenhouse gases created by human activity are making the greenhouse effect much more extreme.

## A global impact

The natural environment is very sensitive. Even a small increase in temperature can have a big impact. Global warming caused by the greenhouse effect is affecting many different parts of the world, including the polar ice caps (see pages 10–13), coasts (see page 11) and coral reefs (see page 17).

Some heat from the Sun bounces straight off the surface of the Earth and back out into space.

atmosphere

# Rising sea levels

Climate change has a significant impact on the seas and oceans. The increase in temperature is causing sea levels to rise and destroying ocean habitats.

The oceans have absorbed **90%** of the extra heat caused by the greenhouse effect.

## Warm water

The rise in temperature on Earth is heating up the ocean. When water warms up, it expands and takes up more space than cool water. This is causing sea levels to rise around the world. Half of the rise in sea levels in the past century is because of warm water expansion.

## Ice sheets

Huge blocks of ice cover the land and the ocean at the Earth's north and south poles. These ice sheets are made up of a huge amount of frozen fresh water. There are also blocks of sea ice, which are formed of frozen salt water.

## Melting ice

Warmer air temperatures are causing the ice sheets to melt. When the ice sheets melt, the liquid water travels into the ocean. This additional water makes the sea levels rise.

Scientists estimate that the sea levels will have risen by 28 to 98 cm by 2100. If all the polar ice melted, sea levels would rise by up to 7 m.

7

## Habitat destruction

As the ice sheets melt, the habitat of many polar animals that live and hunt on the ice, such as polar bears, is being destroyed. Polar bears hunt seals from holes in the sea ice where seals come up to breathe. Without the sea ice, polar bears have fewer opportunities to catch seals to eat, and they are going hungry. Many are starving to death.

*A polar bear lies in wait on the ice for a seal to appear.*

## Dangers

Rising sea levels are causing flooding in low coastal areas. This threatens the homes and businesses of millions of people. By 2100, the homes of 275 million people around the world could be flooded. Most of the people vulnerable to flooding live in south and southeast Asia.

*Flooding is already common in Bangladesh – one of the countries most vulnerable to rising sea levels. By 2050, as many as 25 million people in Bangladesh could be affected.*

## Not enough salt

Melting ice sheets also affect underwater ecosystems, because the melted water that comes off the ice sheets is fresh water. This dilutes the salt water of the ocean. Ocean wildlife, such as sharks, need salt water to survive, so they will be harmed if the water becomes less salty.

# The Greenland ice sheet

The surface of Greenland is covered in the second largest ice sheet on Earth. It is made up of layers of snow packed tightly together. The Greenland ice sheet has already started melting. If it melts entirely, it will have serious consequences around the world.

## FACT FILE

LOCATION:
Greenland

SIZE:
1,710,000 square km

THICKNESS:
Up to 3 km

Greenland

## Icebergs

As the ice sheet melts, large chunks can break away from it. These chunks move into the ocean as icebergs. The icebergs can block the path of ships and cause great damage if the ships collide with them.

## Ice cycle

Every year, the Greenland ice sheet gains ice in the winter from fallen snow. In summer, some ice melts away. However, its average mass shouldn't change too much as it regains in winter what it loses in summer. This is no longer the case, due to climate change. The ice sheet is now losing much more ice than it gains.

**The melting Greenland ice sheet alone is adding 1 mm per year to rising sea levels.**

## Causes

Experts aren't sure why the Greenland ice sheet is melting so quickly. It sits on land, so it should melt more slowly than sea ice, which melts fast when it comes into contact with warm water. Scientists think it may be part of a natural cycle of ice loss and gain, made worse by climate change.

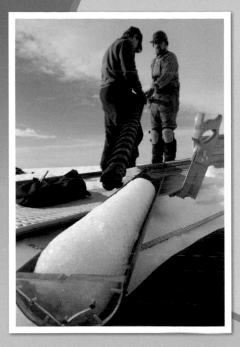

*Scientists are drilling down into the deep ice that formed hundreds of years ago, hoping this research will help them understand why the ice is melting so fast.*

## Dark ice

One reason for the excess melting could be the colour of the ice. When the top layer of ice melts away, it exposes older, darker ice beneath the surface. This ice's dark colour means that it absorbs more light from the Sun and melts more quickly.

*Coloured algae can also grow on the surface of the ice, making it darker and quicker to melt.*

## Weather threats

If the Greenland ice sheet completely melted, the height of the island would be much lower. This would affect air circulation around the Arctic. At the moment, storms 'bounce' off Greenland and back into the ocean. If this didn't happen, the storms would carry on towards other countries in the North Atlantic.

## Protecting the ice

One possible way to preserve the ice could be to wrap it in white blankets. The white colour of the blankets would reflect sunlight away, reducing the amount of ice melted.

# Farming and food

Farming and food supply are closely connected to climate change. The production of some types of food, such as beef, contribute to climate change, while some crops have been negatively affected by global warming.

Animal farming is responsible for 14.5% of all greenhouse gas emissions.

## Cattle farming

Raising cows for their meat, milk and leather contributes to climate change. This is because cows release methane, a greenhouse gas. In small numbers, this wouldn't be an issue. However, the average population of cows on Earth is around one billion, which results in a huge amount of methane.

## Deforestation

Large areas of forest and grassland have been cleared to make room for livestock farms. Deforestation contributes to climate change, as the plants and trees are no longer alive to absorb carbon dioxide from the atmosphere, increasing the greenhouse effect. Plants absorb carbon dioxide as part of photosynthesis, which gives the plants energy to survive.

# Crops

Plants are easily affected by changes in weather caused by climate change. They can be scorched if temperatures are too high, drowned by too much rain or dry out in periods of drought. This can cause entire crops to fail, leaving farmers with no income and whole communities with no food supply.

*These stalks of corn have not developed properly due to drought and very high temperatures.*

## The future of food

Food supply will certainly be affected by future climate change. Many countries will struggle to grow enough food to support their population. This will hit less economically developed countries particularly hard, as they can't afford to buy in food. However, some northern areas, such as Canada, predict that they will be able to grow more crops as temperatures rise.

*Farmers in Malawi struggle to grow crops after years of drought.*

## One small step

**Buy local and seasonal food when possible. Avoid foods that have travelled a long way.**

## Food transportation

In the past, people could only eat food that grew in their local area at certain times of year. This has changed thanks to quick food transportation, which allows us to eat food from around the world all year round. However, the planes, lorries and ships carrying food burn fuel and release greenhouse gases, contributing to climate change.

# Habitats and wildlife

Climate change is having a huge impact on the natural world. Many plants and animals are losing their habitats and food supply, putting them at risk of extinction. Others are on the move, finding new places to live.

## Food chains

Every living thing in an ecosystem is connected through food chains. If just one plant or animal becomes less common or dies out as a result of climate change, it affects every other living thing as well. They may have less food to eat or there may be more predators that eat them. This has a knock-on effect across the entire ecosystem.

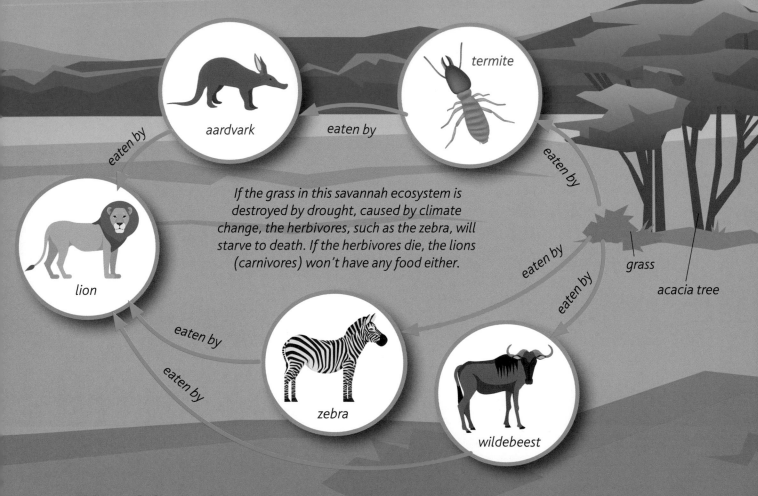

*eaten by*

aardvark    *eaten by*    termite

*eaten by*

*If the grass in this savannah ecosystem is destroyed by drought, caused by climate change, the herbivores, such as the zebra, will starve to death. If the herbivores die, the lions (carnivores) won't have any food either.*

*eaten by*    *eaten by*    grass

lion    acacia tree

*eaten by*    zebra

*eaten by*    wildebeest

## Plant life cycles

Climate change can affect plants' life cycles. Plants are starting to flower earlier in the year as the temperature is warmer. This means that some flowers may not get pollinated, as the insects that pollinate them are not around at the right time. Plants also produce fruit earlier, which may make it hard for animals to survive in autumn, as the fruit that they depend on for food appeared too early.

# Migration

Some animals, such as birds and fish, migrate. They move to different areas at different times of the year, looking for food, warmer temperatures or a mate. Migration is triggered by the seasons, so changes in temperature caused by climate change can confuse animals' migration patterns.

## On the move

Other animals are moving into new areas where it was once too cold for them to survive, because of climate change. This is affecting the food chains in these habitats, as the ecosystem adjusts to include new animals that need to find food. New species are also being produced as plants and animals reproduce with species that move into their habitat.

*The pizzly bear is a mix between a polar bear and a grizzly bear. These species have mixed for the first time because polar bears have moved south into grizzly bear territory to look for food, as global warming destroys their ice habitat.*

## An acidic ocean

The ocean absorbs about 30 per cent of the carbon dioxide in the atmosphere. As the amount of $CO_2$ in the atmosphere increases, so does the level of $CO_2$ in the ocean. This is making the ocean more acidic. This acidity damages the shells of ocean animals, such as clams and oysters.

*Coral is unable to grow and eventually dissolves in acidic water.*

coral

clams

# FOCUS ON

# Sea turtles

Sea turtles are particularly vulnerable to climate change, as they depend on both ocean and beach habitats at different points of their life. If global warming continues, these animals, and the ecosystems in which they live, could be at serious risk.

## FACT FILE

LOCATION:
All oceans, except the polar regions

NUMBER OF SPECIES: 7

THREATS:
Climate change, habitat loss, poaching

## Sea and beach

Adult sea turtles spend most of their lives at sea. They come to land to lay their eggs on beaches every few years. Having access to safe beaches where their eggs can be laid and hatch is key to the survival of sea turtles.

## Beach destruction

Rising sea levels are already destroying the beaches where sea turtles lay their eggs, leaving the sea turtles with nowhere to go. Sea turtle eggs are also washed away by waves, which are coming higher up the beach than ever before.

## Coral reefs

Hawksbill sea turtles often live in coral reefs. They feed on sea sponges that grow among the coral. The destruction of coral reefs, caused by the acidification of the ocean (see page 17), is threatening these turtles that depend on coral reefs for food.

*The Hawksbill sea turtle uses its sharp beak to grab bites of sea sponge.*

**99%** of sea turtles born on one Australian island are female. In the 1970s, only **83%** were born female.

## Hot sand

If sea turtle eggs are laid in hot sand, the turtle that hatches is likely to be female. Rising temperatures are causing a very high number of certain sea turtles to be born female. In the short term, this can help sea turtle numbers, as there are more females who can lay eggs. However, if too few male turtles are born, not enough sea turtles will be able to reproduce.

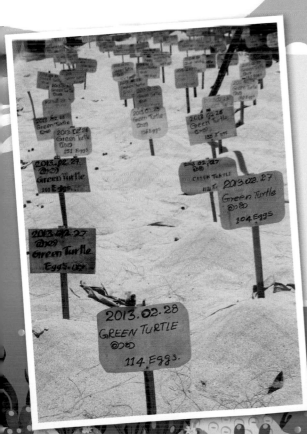

## Protecting turtles

As well as working to reduce climate change, people are protecting sea turtles in more direct ways. Sea turtle nesting beaches are being built up to stop them being eroded by rising sea levels. Conservationists are moving turtle nests to shady or protected areas where the temperature of the sand can be controlled.

*These sea turtle eggs have been reburied in a safe place.*

# Desertification

Desertification is when fertile land is destroyed and becomes dry land where nothing can grow. This process happens as a result of climate change and human activity.

Plants are killed off by high temperatures caused by climate change.

Humans cut down trees for their wood or clear land for livestock farming.

Soil can lose its nutrients if farmers don't fertilise it, so plants can't grow in it any longer.

**LOSS OF PLANTS**

## Soil erosion

Plant roots help to hold soil together. Once plants and their roots are gone, soil is much more vulnerable to erosion. The top layers of soil are easily blown away by wind or washed away by water. This exposes lower, less fertile layers of soil where no plants can grow.

## One small step

It's important to give nutrients back to the soil. Keep a compost bin of food waste at home or at school and fertilise the soil with the compost you make. Find a link on page 31.

## Grassland grazing

For many years, people thought that grazing livestock contributed to desertification in grassland areas. They believed that the animals ate too many plants, leading to soil erosion. So, they removed the livestock, but the desertification continued. Later, people realised that the grassland ecosystem depends on grazing animals. The animals fertilise the soil with their waste and help to mix up the soil when they are migrating or running away from predators. However, too much livestock can overgraze grasslands and contribute to climate change in other ways (see page 14).

## Solving the problem

Desertified lands are home to about one-sixth of the world's population. However, nearly all of these people live in less economically developed countries. It can be hard for the governments of these countries to find the resources to address the issue of desertification.

## Causing climate change

Desertification isn't just a consequence of climate change. It's also a cause of climate change. Plants take in carbon dioxide. When plants are lost in the process of desertification, there are fewer plants available to absorb carbon dioxide. This increases the amount of carbon dioxide in the atmosphere.

*A desertified area in Burkina Faso, Africa.*

## Fear and fighting

Desertification can lead to conflict. When land becomes a desert, crops can no longer be grown and water sources dry up. Shortages of food and water in desertified areas can lead to fighting, as people argue over resources. Desertification can also force people to leave their homes and become refugees.

*Many people in Somalia have fled to refugee camps in Kenya, escaping violence from a civil war and food shortages caused by desertification and drought.*

21

# Desertification in China

Desertification is a serious problem in northern China. Deserts are quickly approaching major cities, threatening homes and affecting the country's food supply.

## FACT FILE

**LOCATION:**
Asia

**% OF LAND THAT IS DESERT OR DESERTIFIED:**
27.4%

**NUMBER AFFECTED:**
400 million people

## History

Desertification has been an issue in China since the 1950s, when forests and fields were destroyed to build new cities. Workers built on the cleared land and used the wood for construction. The undeveloped cleared land became desert.

The Gobi Desert in China absorbs
**3,600 square km**
of grassland every year. It is the fastest-growing desert on Earth.

Removing the trees has made it easier for the wind to carry sand to new areas and for existing deserts to expand.

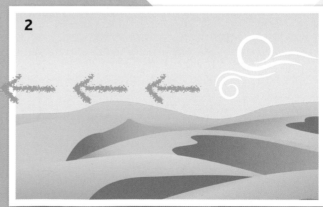

## Sandstorms

Sandstorms are becoming more common in northern China as a result of desertification. In some areas, they happen three to ten times a month. Sandstorms damage crops and cause pollution. In China's already polluted cities, they make air quality and visibility even worse.

*The sand and pollution in the air over Beijing, China, makes visibility very poor.*

## Food shortages

The loss of farmland results in a decrease in food supply, as farmers have nowhere to grow crops. China's population is also increasing, which puts even more pressure on the food supply. China may experience food shortages if desertification continues at its current rate.

## People

An increasing number of people in China are environmental refugees, who are forced to leave their homes because of desertification. Some of these refugees are farmers who have lost their farmland. With no way to earn a living, they are forced to move away in search of work.

## Finding solutions

Since 1978, the Chinese government has been trying to slow down desertification by planting a huge line of trees called the Great Green Wall of China. These trees were intended to stop the Gobi Desert from expanding. However, most of the trees have died as there isn't enough water in the soil to support them. The surviving trees have only managed to stop desertification in some areas.

Only **15%** of the
**66 billion trees**
planted in the Great Green Wall
of China have survived.

# Extreme weather

Scientists believe that climate change is making extreme weather, such as hurricanes, heat waves and heavy rain, more common and more extreme. These events can have a devastating impact.

## Hurricanes

Hurricanes, also known as tropical cyclones or typhoons, are the strongest tropical storms. They are powered by warm, wet air that sits near the surface of the ocean.

❶ Warm, wet air rises from the surface of the ocean.

❷ This air condenses higher up to form clouds.

❸ An area of low pressure forms near the surface of the water.

❹ The low-pressure area sucks in more warm air, which rises up and is pushed out at the top.

❺ Air quickly flows around the low-pressure area in a spiral.

This process happens more quickly and more frequently when the air and water is warmer, which is happening as a result of global warming.

## Rainfall

Warm air can hold more water than cool air. This means that warm clouds carry more water and drop more rain. As a result, the higher temperatures caused by global warming will result in more rainfall.

**Air can hold 7% more water for every 1°C increase in temperature.**

*flooding*

*Almond trees in California can usually survive periods of flooding and drought.*

*drought*

## Drought

Warm air makes water evaporate more quickly. This can cause soil to dry out, resulting in periods of drought. Some areas, such as California, USA, are already experiencing alternating periods of droughts and flooding because of climate change.

## Heat waves

As the Earth gets warmer, periods of extreme heat are becoming more common. In early 2018, southern Australia experienced a heat wave so severe that the roads melted in some places. Heat waves also increase the risk of dangerous forest fires. People who live near the already warm equator are at risk of deadly humid heat waves, in which the body can't cool down, as the air is too wet for sweat to evaporate.

## Cold weather

Some scientists are concerned that rising temperatures in the Arctic are destroying the polar vortex – a circle of strong winds that keeps cold air trapped in the Arctic. If the polar vortex were destroyed, the cold Arctic air would be free to travel across the northern hemisphere, causing freezing temperatures and heavy snow.

**One-third** of the world faces deadly heat waves because of climate change.

# FOCUS ON Hurricane Harvey

In August 2017, Hurricane Harvey hit the Caribbean and south coast of the USA. It was the wettest storm in US history, probably as a result of climate change. The heavy rains caused serious damage across the US state of Texas.

## FACT FILE

LOCATION:
**The Caribbean and southern USA**

MAXIMUM RECORDED RAINFALL: **130 cm**

HIGHEST FLOOD LEVEL: **3 m**

## On the move

Hurricane Harvey formed in the east of the Caribbean. It then travelled northwest, hitting a few Caribbean islands and crossing the southeast coast of Mexico. The hurricane paused over the state of Texas for a few days, dropping huge amounts of rain. It then moved northeast towards Louisiana before dying away.

## Wind and rain

The hurricane brought extreme weather, from 200 kph winds to extremely heavy rain. Scientists believe that climate change increased the rainfall of Hurricane Harvey by nearly 20 per cent, as warmer air can hold more water.

## Flooding

Hurricane Harvey resulted in serious floods. This was partly due to the heavy rain, but also to a storm surge – a side effect of the storm that made sea levels rise along the coast. Reservoirs built to trap rainwater burst their banks and flooded, which made the problem even worse.

*People use boats to get around in the flooded streets of Houston, Texas, after Hurricane Harvey.*

The weight of the water in Houston made the city temporarily sink by 2 cm.

## Houston

The city of Houston, Texas, was particularly affected by Hurricane Harvey. It is a low-lying city, which was quickly flooded by the storm surge. It is also built on clay soil, which water does not drain away through easily. Many other low-lying coastal cities around the world will be similarly affected by storms in the future.

## Evacuation

A state of emergency was called as Hurricane Harvey moved closer to the USA. Around 30,000 people evacuated their homes and moved to higher ground to escape the storm. However, not everyone was able to get away. The emergency services carried out over 13,000 rescues and 107 people were killed.

## Recovery

The damage caused by Hurricane Harvey in the USA will cost more than US $125 billion to repair. Hundreds of thousands of homes were flooded or damaged by high winds. Many roads, businesses and public services, such as schools, were also affected.

*High winds and heavy rain pulled away the wall of this house in Texas.*

# Stopping climate change

Solving the problem of climate change involves stopping temperatures from rising further and gradually bringing them back down to a natural level. Everyone has a part to play in this process, from governments and businesses to individual people.

## Fighting back

The most important step towards fighting climate change is to stop more damage from being done. To do so, we need to reduce the amount of greenhouse gases in the atmosphere. We can this by burning fewer fossil fuels and reducing cattle farming. We can also plant more trees and prevent deforestation, so that there are more plants to absorb extra carbon dioxide from the atmosphere.

## Climate change agreements

Many countries around the world have signed climate change agreements that promise they will reduce the amount of greenhouse gases they release. In theory, this should help to control climate change around the world. However, as countries set their own targets and receive no penalties if they don't meet them, these agreements may not help much.

## Climate change deniers

A few people have doubts about climate change. Some people believe that the climate is changing naturally, while others think that it isn't changing at all. However, as nearly all climate scientists state that evidence suggests that humans are responsible for climate change, it's interesting to think why people might deny that climate change is happening. Some might benefit from the sale of fossil fuels, while others might want to clear land to start a farm.

## Catching carbon

Scientists are also experimenting with new techniques to control climate change. One is to turn carbon dioxide into a liquid and inject it deep into the Earth in empty oil or water reserves. The carbon dioxide would then be trapped underground. However, this has not been tested long term and there is a risk it might escape, damage the surrounding rock or have other negative effects.

*Taking the train rather than flying is one way of producing fewer greenhouse gases.*

### One small step

Solving climate change can seem scary and overwhelming. However, there are things that we can all do to help. Walk or cycle rather than taking the car. Write a letter to your local MP and find out what is being done locally to reduce the use of fossil fuels. These small steps will help to protect the planet.

# Glossary

**condense** when gas turns into a liquid

**conflict** fighting between different groups

**conservationist** someone whose job it is to protect nature

**decompose** to break down

**deforestation** cutting down trees and clearing the land

**dilute** to make a liquid weaker by adding another liquid to it

**drought** a period when there isn't enough water

**ecosystem** all the living things in an area

**erosion** the breaking down of rocks and movement of sand and soil

**evaporate** when a liquid turns into a gas

**fossil fuel** a fuel that comes from the ground, such as coal, oil or gas

**graze** to eat grass

**greenhouse gas** a gas that traps heat in the atmosphere, such as carbon dioxide

**Industrial Revolution** a period in the eighteenth and nineteenth centuries in which products started to be made in factories, rather than by hand

**livestock** animals that are raised for their meat or other products

**photosythesis** the process by which plants use energy from the Sun to create their own food

**pollination** the process in which plants are fertilised and produce new seeds

**refugee** someone who has been forced to leave their home

**renewable** describes something that can be reproduced and will not run out

# Further reading

*Go Green!* by Liz Gogerly (Franklin Watts, 2018)

*The Energy We Use* by Georgia Amson-Bradshaw (Wayland, 2018)

*Climate Change (Can We Really Stop It?)* by Philip Steele (Wayland, 2017)

# Websites

climatekids.nasa.gov/climate-change-meaning/
Get the facts about climate change.

www.explainthatstuff.com/globalwarmingforkids.html
Find out more about global warming.

www.earthday.org/climate-change-quiz/
Take a quiz about climate change.

www.bbc.co.uk/gardening/gardening_with_children/homegrownprojects_compost.shtml
Learn how to make a compost bin.

# Index